67 Lateral Thinking Puzzles

Games And Riddles To Kill Time And Build Brain Cells

Karen J. Bun

Table of Contents

Introduction

Firstly, thank you for purchasing "67 Lateral
Thinking Puzzles!" I sincerely hope you enjoy the
following lateral puzzles provided in this book.
Lateral puzzles are an excellent way to expand and
grow your mind creatively. These puzzles are not
simply to be solved by logical, step-by-step
thinking. Instead, they are designed to mind-boggle
you with a wide array of different possibilities!
Originally termed by Dr. Edward De Bono in 1967,
lateral thinking is a unique approach to problem-
solving. This is done by using concepts that are not
entirely obvious to figure out the answer. Edward
described lateral thinking as the description of a
process. The said process entails a creative, talented
approach that considers factors that are not
necessarily facts or even logical in some cases. You
may even say lateral thinking is a reliance on your
gut feeling, or following a mystical inclination that
guides you towards what may be the right answer,
or in some cases, what may be an alternative to an
already existing answer. In the following puzzles
you will be given a scenario with very little, but just
enough information to speculate on what the
answer may be. Even a "wrong" answer can be an
interesting, thought-provoking one! For your peace
of mind, however, the answers to said puzzles will
be provided in the back of this book for you to
look at once you've finished speculating. They will

all be numbered accordingly from 1 to 67 so that you can match the puzzle to the puzzle answer. Now, feel free to keep reading and enjoy!

Puzzles

1. John's Trucking Disaster

John's Trucking company delivers to all the local businesses and has been doing so reliably for years. John's truck drivers travel the same route on the same roads every day without running into any issues, and they are all reliable drivers. Despite this, John's business is in need of money, and he needs to ask some of those drivers to work overtime during the holidays. As a way to make more profit this year, John decided that on Christmas Day, his drivers would continue to deliver goods. So, on Christmas Day, John sends off a few of his workers to deliver to those of the businesses that were still open on holiday. Near the end of the day, John receives a phone call informing him one of his delivery trucks has struck a bridge, and the truck has been severely damaged. Why and how did this happen on this particular day despite the fact the drivers were traveling the same route they always do previously without issue?

2. Mystery Weight Loss

A woman willingly enters an enclosed room by herself. She reaches and presses a button, and she can instantly lose twenty pounds. How was she able to do this by the simple press of a button? And where is she?

3. The Man In The Dark Room

A man sits in a dark room, enjoying himself and feeling rather entertained. In a matter of moments, he suddenly stops breathing and cannot speak. Soon after, he can speak again, and his breathing returns to normal without the Heimlich maneuver being done to help him. What happened to him and where is he?

4. The Burglar

A wanted man committed several crimes for several months. He stole from several businesses during those months and took a decent amount of money from all of them. On one of these occasions, he was caught on the surveillance tape, and the recording was shown to the police investigating. On this tape, it clearly showed the man's face, and posters were posted all around town asking for information on the wanted man. The footage was even shown on the local TV news, asking for anyone with information on the man to catch him. However, when the man walked by the two officers aware of these burglaries, they did not react whatsoever. They barely even look his way. Why was that?

5. The Car Accident

Just alongside a large hill, more than 45 cars were caught up in a traffic accident. The pile-up was very catastrophic. Some cars were turned over, while others had flown on top of other cars. The accident was so large that a firetruck, a police vehicle and military vehicles were involved in the crash. How could this accident come to be?

6. Stranger In The Car

Due to a disturbance, a man helps his wife into their car, and they race desperately down the road at the top speed possible. They eventually have to stop, and the man leaves the vehicle and runs. When he returns just a few short minutes later, his wife is barely conscious and is with a stranger who is beside her in the seat. What happened to his wife while he was gone?

7. Poisoned Iced Tea

Two best friends go out to dinner together. Both decide to order iced tea with their meal. While one drinks very slowly and talks to her friend for a few minutes between sips, the other finishes her drink very quickly and ends up drinking five iced teas while the other girl is still on her first glass. Afterward, they find out that they were poisoned, but the girl who drank the most iced tea suffers no illness while the other is taken to the hospital. Why would the girl who drank the most iced tea experience no symptoms of being poisoned while the other required immediate medical attention?

8.   Poisoned Glass

As a challenge, you are given a total of 1000 glasses. Out of all of those glasses, one contains poison, which therefore causes the juice to taste bitter. You are tasked with finding the one glass out of 1000 that contains the poison. You are provided with an antidote once you do find it, so sipping the poison to identify it is no issue. What method can be used to take the least amount of sips possible in order to find the poisoned glass without having to sip each and every one until you find it?

9.   The Forgotten Book

A lady came up to a man behind a counter and gave him a book. The man thanked her, and then said, "That will be four dollars." The lady nods and gives him the money. She then proceeds to leave without the book in hand. The man watches her leave but made no move to call her back. Why is this?

10.   The Twins

One day, Carol celebrated her birthday. Two days later, her older twin, Cheryl, celebrated her birthday as well. What scenario would allow for this to be possible?

11.   The Cowboy

A cowboy rode into town on a Monday. He went and rented a room to stay for three entire days and nights. When he finished his stay, he left on Monday. How did he manage to do that?

12.   The Sentencing

A young, foolish teenager is put on trial and is found guilty of a minor charge. The Judge, deciding to have some fun with the man, tells him, "You can say one sentence to defend yourself in your sentencing. If you lie, you will be locked away. If you tell us the truth, you will be set free and only given a warning." What should the young man say to gain his freedom?

13. Wrong Hotel Room

A woman was settled in her hotel room when she heard a knock at her door. Confused, as she wasn't expecting anyone, she gets up and answers the door. On the other side, there was a man who seemed surprised to see her answer. "My apologies, madam! I thought this was my room! Sorry to disturb you." He left immediately after and the woman returned into her room to call hotel security. Why would she suspect anything?

14. The Triangle

Here are two triangles made up of equal parts. However, the bottom one is missing a box. How is this possible?

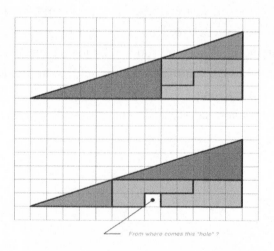

From where comes this "hole" ?

15. True Love At A Funeral

A young lady attended her mother's funeral. While she was there, she met a mysterious love interest. She was utterly charmed by him, as he was the man of her dreams and she has been on her own for a long time. She falls madly in love with him instantly just after one day of the meeting. A few days after the funeral the girl murders her own sister. What reason would she have of doing this?

16. The Murderer

The police department receives a phone call providing an anonymous tip about a suspected murderer, stating that the murderer is hiding out in a house playing a game of poker. The police immediately raid the house mentioned in the tip. They do not, however, know anything about the appearance of the suspected murderer. All they know is that he is a man, and his name is Michael. Upon entering the house, they see a taxi driver, a blacksmith, a plumber, and a fireman all playing poker. Without hesitating, the police officers arrest the fireman without a word or interaction with the others. How would they know that the fireman was the murderer without knowing anything about the murderer's appearance?

17. Thirsty

A man lies in his own bed and passes away in the comfort of his own home due to thirst. Why would he allow this to happen?

18. Clean Faces

Two best friends, Tom and Henry, are playing on the school playground during recess. When recess is over, and the bell rings, the two boys run back to class. On their way a giant gust of wind causes a mass of dirt to be thrown in both of their faces. Tom's face is absolutely filthy, while Henry's is still miraculously clean. However, it is Henry that rushes to the bathroom to clean his face, while Tom returns to class without doing so. Assuming that both boys care equally about their own hygiene, why would they each react this way?

19. Fingerprints

Almost every single night, a man enters the police station after hours and destroys hundreds upon hundreds of fingerprints. Even so, that man has never been charged or caught of a crime. How is this possible?

20. Pool Balls

You have been given the following pool balls.

Using the numbers shown in the following picture

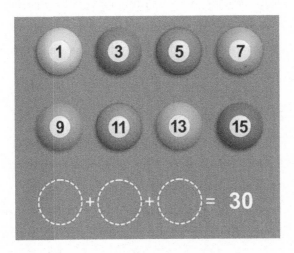

(1, 3, 5, 7, 9, 11, 13, and 15), you need to select three in order to add to 30. What balls can you use?

21. The Philosopher

A careless philosopher forgot to wind up his clock. He now has no way of attaining the time as he doesn't prefer to keep up with technology and prefers to live with little influence from the outside world. He has no radio, no TV, no telephone, no internet, or any other means of getting the time besides walking to his friend's house to get it from him. He sets out to do this and walks to his friend's house. It is a straight desert road, and the travel is only a few miles. He stays there for the night and walks home the following morning. He is then able to set his clock to the correct time. The philosopher did not bring anything to this friend's house in order to keep track of time in any way, nor did he have his friend time him. How was he able to estimate the time that passed on his walk home from his friend's in order to set the clock?

22. Found Guilty

A man is brought to court after being accused of murdering his wife after his wife was reported missing and has now been missing for a month. The man claims that his wife has left him, leaving nothing behind so that he would not be able to find her and that he is not guilty of murder. As part of his defense, his lawyer asks everyone present to look to the back. "To prove that my client is not guilty, I have asked his wife to enter the doors in just a minute to prove that she has, in fact, not killed!" The entire jury, the judge, and everyone hearing the case looks to the door, only to see no one enter. After a moment, the lawyer claims, "See! This only proves that you are uncertain that my client could have killed his wife. Otherwise, you would not have bothered looking!" Almost immediately after, the jury all decides that the accused man is guilty. Why is that?

23. Millionaire

A nice gentleman named Mr. Johnson buys up $5 worth of packages full of food and supplies from the United States, only to sell them for a mere $1 in Africa to those in need. He continues doing this for a very long time in order to help out the country. He eventually goes on to become a Millionaire with this plan. How does he manage this?

24. A Load of Wood

Driving down the road, a man miraculously came across a man driving a large truck with a load of wood in the back. His truckload contained wood that was neither straight nor crooked. How is this possible?

25. The Short Line

You are provided with this chalkboard with the line already drawn on in chalk. You are tasked with making this line shorter, but you may not erase

any part of the line. How will you do it?

26. Rectangular House

A man decided to build a house, giving each and every side of the house a fantastic view facing south for his family to look out. After finishing this house, he goes outside and comes face to face with a bear. What kind of bear is it?

27. The Window Cleaner

A window cleaner is working on the 34th floor of a massive skyscraper. While cleaning the windows, he accidentally falls. In this instance, he is wearing absolutely no safety equipment. He does not have a harness and has nothing to slow or soften his fall. However, despite this, he sustains no injuries whatsoever. How did he manage not to get injured from this terrible fall?

28. Three Rooms

You come to three rooms and have to choose to open one of their doors and go inside. The first is filled with flames, the second is filled with tigers who have not eaten in three years, and the third and last room is filled with three hitmen all tasked with terminating you. Which room is the wisest to choose?

29. Three Days

You must find a way to say three consecutive days without saying Monday, Wednesday, or Friday in any of the combinations. How could you do this while still using only English words?

30. The Goldfish

A young girl has a pet goldfish that she adores very much. One day she looks in the bowl and finds that the fish is swimming very weakly and has lost all its energy. Devastated, she takes the goldfish to the vet to help her beloved pet regain its strength. The vet takes a look at her goldfish and quickly returns with the goldfish swimming much better. The girl was thrilled, but this seems suspicious. How did the vet manage to get the goldfish swimming well again?

31. Billy

Little, four-year-old Billy, had both of his parents pass away recently. His new caretaker decided to put Billy on a train on his own to get to his new home in the country. Unfortunately, Billy could not speak or write and could not tell anyone on the train his destination so that they can make sure he gets there on his own. Since this is the case, his guardian writes his destination on a little note and tie it on a string around his neck. Despite this note, Billy never manages to get to his destination. Why is this?

32. Forecast

A man sits at home and watches the weather forecast on his TV. It is just after midnight that the man hears they are expecting rain for the next two days straight, but after 72 hours it will be bright, sunny and warm again. The man laughs and says, "They're wrong again!" How could he predict that for sure? Is he psychic?

33. East and West

While in the North Pole, it is absolutely impossible to look North. The same goes for the South Pole, where it is impossible to look South. With this being the case, where in the world would you have to be in order to be able to look North or South, but not be able to look East or West?

34. Fallen Man

A detective is called to a possible murder scene. Once he arrives, he sees that a man has fallen from an abandoned building, presumably from one of the many windows. His colleagues argue that the man likely did this to himself and this is not a case of murder. The detective pondered on this and traveled inside the building to investigate. He stood on the first floor in front of the window that faces the man and lits a cigarette. After a while, he puts out his cigarette, opens the window and throws it out before closing it again. He does this on the second floor as well as the third floor. After this, he returns back to his colleagues certain that the man was indeed murdered. How did he find this out during his smoke break?

35. The Strings

You hold two different strings of different lengths. You also have a book of matches. If you lit one end of the longer string it will burn for about

10 minutes. If the shorter string is burned it will take only about 1 minute. Using these strings you have to attempt to measure precisely 5 and a half minutes of time. There are a few tools you are unable to use as well. You do not have scissors or anything to cut the string. You also do not have the ability to bend the string correctly in half as it is too rigid. You also cannot accurately estimate the half point of either of the strings just by looking at them because it would still not be entirely accurate. How can you measure the five minutes and thirty seconds?

36. The Wine Bottle

You have both a used wine bottle and the cork left over. If you were to put a small coin within the bottle and insert the cork back into the neck of the bottle, how would you be able to retrieve that coin without breaking the bottle or removing the cork again?

37. The Coffee and the Fly

A woman walks into a cafe and sits down at one of the booths. Soon enough, a waitress comes by and takes her order. She asks for only a cup of coffee. Shortly after the waitress returns with the coffee and heads back to the kitchen. A few minutes later, the woman notices that a fly has found its way into her coffee cup. Politely, the woman motions the waitress to come back and asks for another fresh cup of coffee. The waitress takes her cup and returns to the kitchen. A few minutes later she returns, saying, "There you go. I poured you a new cup of coffee. No fly this time." She leaves the cup on the table and turns to head back to the kitchen. She only makes a few steps before her customer calls her back. "Hey! This is the same cup! You only removed the fly and gave me the same one!" While assuming that the coffee is still hot and the coffee machine is not in view of the customer, how would she be able to tell it was the same coffee?

38. Blindfolded Scott

A blindfolded boy named Scott sits in front of a rotating tray. The tray contains four identical individual glasses. Some are upside down, and others are right side up. However, he is not aware of which is which in this situation. The glasses are placed in rows of two, forming a square. A bartender named Mary challenges Scott to rearrange all the glasses so that they all match and are all either right side up or upside down. However, he does have some rules to follow. Any two glasses may be touched in order to see which way they are placed. Mary shall help him locate and touch the glasses. Scott can go ahead and flip either both glasses, one of them, or flip neither. Mary will then spin the tray to a random number of degrees to provide new and random positions of the glasses. This will continue until Scott manages to get all four glasses in the same orientation, at which point Mary will let him know. In this scenario, Scott does not want to exceed five turns of the tray before getting the right answer. What strategy can he use to do this?

39. Manholes

Manhole covers are all made in a circular shape as opposed to a square because they have a commanding advantage. What are the circular-shaped covers preferred for?

40. The Long Fishing Rod

A man purchases a brand new fishing rod and needs to take the bus home. He stands in line and attempts to board the bus. Unfortunately, they measure the rod, and he is informed that it is too long to bring on the bus. The maximum length of an item is 4 feet, and his fishing rod is 5 feet. The man sadly returns to the store to return the item. Thankfully, the cashier proposes a smart way to be still able to board with the fishing rod. The man is skeptical as he does not want to break or bend the fishing rod to do this. However, the cashier is able to suggest a way that avoids doing this. What is his proposal?

41. The Chemist

A chemist is murdered in his lab. The crime scene leaves no solid clues for his murder except for one. The chemist left a piece of paper behind. On that paper, was a list of several different substances. These substances were nickel, carbon, oxygen, lanthanum, and sulfur. After collecting this piece of evidence, the police looked for their next clue. They checked with everyone that came by that lab that entire day. His nephew Nicolas came by, his lab partner Gina came by, his wife came by, and his friend James came by. They did not even have to call them in for questioning. The officers knew immediately who the murderer was. It was Nicolas. How did they come to this conclusion so quickly?

42. Man in the Field

A man mysteriously lies face down in a field, deceased, and wearing a backpack. A few moments before his death, he became aware of his approaching demise. However, there were no objects of importance in the field nor on him or in his backpack. He was not killed by a person or an animal, and he was perfectly healthy and not ailed in any way. He did not die of old age, stroke, or of any health condition or allergy. He was also not killed by a lightning strike or any other act of God. So, how did he end up dying and how did he know it would happen?

43. The Wish

A manservant works for his master tirelessly for thirty years. He is loyal and a good man to his master. After those thirty years, his master falls ill and is certain that he will not recover. With his faithful manservant at his side, he admits that he has extraordinary powers and would like to grant his servant one wish before he passes away as a thank you for his service. The manservant is very thankful, but cannot decide on the spot so his master gives him one day to decide on what he would like to wish. He goes home and speaks to his wife about it, who then is overjoyed at the possibility. "Wish for a son! We have been childless for too many years! Now is our chance!" The manservant considers this. Then, he goes and speaks with his mother, who is blind. She is also overjoyed and says, "Please, son! Ask for my sight back so that I may see the world again!" The manservant also considers this. Then, he speaks with his father, who has been awfully poor his whole life and is now too old to make any sort of living. "Please, son! Ask for the riches our family has always had to live without!" The manservant considers this as well and is torn. What will he end up choosing? Is there an option that allows him to make everyone happy?

44. Mountain Trip Accident

Mr. and Mrs. Gold took a vacation to the mountains for their anniversary. They hiked together to the top of the mountain. Unfortunately, only Mr. Gold would end up returning. Upon his return he reports the death of his wife, stating that his wife accidentally fell to her death from the edge of a cliff during their hike and he was unable to save her in time. The police officers end up arresting Mr. Gold shortly after searching his hotel room for the murder of his wife, has found substantial evidence that he intended to murder his wife. What could they have seen that suggested this?

45. St. Ives

On his way to St. Ives, a man happens upon a plentiful family. He came across a man with 6 wives, each carrying 6 sacks filled with 6 mother cats, all with 6 kittens each. That makes one man with plenty of wives and sacks filled with cats and kittens in tow. How many of them are going to St. Ives?

46. The Equal Squares

You are given a square and told to divide it into four different equal parts. There are two simple enough ways to do this as you can see below. However, there are 8 other different ways to do this. What are those other ways?

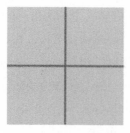 

47. Truck Driver

A police officer is driving on the highway and notices a truck driver clearly traveling in the wrong direction. Instead of pulling over and setting him straight, he ignores him and keeps going. Why would he ignore this?

48. Plane Crash

A terrible plane crash occurred in the mountains. Forty people were on board, none surviving. They were found later the same day, but no survivors were buried. Why is that?

49. Snowball

A man sat alone in the comfort of his home in front of his fireplace. It was a very cold, winter evening, and snow covered his entire backyard. As he sat and relaxed, he was suddenly disturbed by a snowball that came crashing through his window. Understandably angry that he was now exposed to the cold, he ran up to the window and saw three of the neighborhood boys in his backyard. They were all laughing and running away as they joked around with each other. The man was able to identify the boys as three brothers by the names Jack Smith, Mark Smith, and Tom Smith. As they were already running away and he didn't feel like chasing them, the man closed up the broken window and went to bed. The very next morning, he went out to retrieve his newspaper and found a paper note stuck to his door. It said, "? Smith. He threw the snowball and broke your window." The man instantly knew from this note which brother it was that broke his window. How did he know?

50. The Sand Smuggler

A strange man crosses the Mexican border regularly every single day while only riding a bicycle. Every time he does, he carries two bags full of sand with him. The customs officers check the bag, only to find only sand every single time. They suspect that he is smuggling something but to their frustration, they can never find any proof, so he always gets away with it. What is he hiding?

51. Guilty Husband

A man has just murdered his wife. When he returned home, he received a call from the police stating that his wife has been murdered and her body was only found at the scene of the crime. The man fakes his shock, and the police ask him to come to the scene of the crime right away. The man jumps in his car and gets there as soon as possible, only to be arrested the moment he arrives for the murder of his wife. How did the police know it was him?

52. Who Stole The Money?

A man left a $500 bill on his dresser before leaving for his daily routine. When he came home that night, he was irritated to find that the $500 was now gone. He had three employees that could be responsible: the cook, the maid, and the electrician. He went to question the cook first, who claimed that he indeed did see the $500 bill and put it under a book for safekeeping. The man returned to his dresser and saw the book there. Looking under it, he saw that it was no longer there! He then went to question the maid. She immediately claimed that she moved the bill inside the book between the first and second page while she was cleaning his dresser and saw it there. The man went back and checked the book, and saw nothing there. He then spoke with the electrician, who later claimed he saw it poking out of the book and moved it to page 2 and 3 for safekeeping. Enraged, the man immediately fires the electrician and demands his money back. How did he know it was him?

53. Two Cars

Two cars are traveling down the center of town. One of them is a man driving a little red car. The man driving the red car overtakes the black car as it is traveling too slow for his liking. The driver, while doing this, misjudged the amount of time he had to pass before he would get in the way of oncoming traffic. The black car swerves into a local shop to avoid an accident and crashes through the window. The red car swerves as well out of the way of the oncoming traffic and successfully avoids all the oncoming cars without harming himself. In the black car, however, there is one dead man found after the accident. Despite this, the driver of the green car is not charged with manslaughter. Why not?

54. Cell Window

Carl is locked in a jail cell. The ground is made of dirt, and he has a shovel. He also has a cell window, but it is just out of reach at his height. Carl is trying to plan an escape that takes less than two days because he will not have access to food or water during his journey. He considered digging a tunnel in the dirt, but it will still take more than two days, and he will not make it. How else will he be able to escape?

55. Captain's Missing Ring

A Japanese ship is leaving port. The Captain grabs some oil to grease up some parts of the ship. Before he leaves, he takes off his ring and leaves it behind so that he won't lose it or damage it. He leaves it on his dresser in his cabin. He returns ten minutes later only to find that his ring is gone. He asks his crew about the missing ring. His cook says "I was busy in the kitchen, making tonight's dinner for everyone in the crew." He speaks to the engineer. He says, "I was working hard in the engine room to make sure everything was running smoothly before we leave port." He talks to the seaman then. He says, "I was on the mast correcting the flag. Someone had accidentally

attached it upside down and had to be corrected."
The Captain immediately knows who is lying about
their whereabouts. Who is lying? How did he
know?

56. First Day of School

On the first day back to school, the science
teacher was murdered. All four suspects turned out
to be all fellow employees at the school as no one
else had entered the building that early in the
morning. The first suspect was the principal. He
claims that he was in his office at the time of the
crime, preparing for the new school year. The
second suspect was the history teacher. She says
that she was preparing for her midterm tests to give
to her students. The third suspect was the
landscaper. He says that he was mowing the lawn
before the students arrive. The fourth and final
suspect was the Track and Field coach. She says
that she was setting up to do some drills outside
with her students. The police know immediately
after questioning everyone who is guilty. It is the
history teacher. How did they figure this out?

57. The Princess's Hand In Marriage

A poor man with no land or anything to his name
falls in love with the princess of the Kingdom he
lives in. Desperate for her love, he courts her in
secret, and they fall in love with each other. They

come to the King, her father, together and present her wish to marry him. The King is not at all pleased with this proposal but does not want to appear unfair and then proposes an alternative. He will allow the poor man to marry his daughter if he wins a game of chance. He will put two pieces of paper in a bowl. One will say, "Exile." If he picks this one, he will be banished from the Kingdom and never see the Princess ever again. The other piece of paper will say, "Marriage." If he picks this one, the marriage will continue. The poor man happily agrees as he believes any chance is better than no chance at all. However, later that night, the hopeful man overhears the King talking to one of his men. He says, "I will be writing 'Exile' on both of those papers. There's no way that man deserves my daughter's hand in marriage!" The man is unaffected and doesn't lose his confidence as he is sure he knows how to turn this in his favor. What does he do to earn the Princess's hand in marriage regardless of the King working against him?

58. Teaspoons of Sugar

You are given three cups, sugar, and a teaspoon. You are tasked with distributing 10 teaspoons of sugar in three different cups. The rule is that there has to be an odd amount of teaspoons in each of the cups. How can you do this while still adding up to 10, an even number?

59. Haircut

A man arrives in a small town and is in desperate need of a haircut. Since he is in such a small town, they only have two barbers across the street from each other. He has to decide between the two by guessing who would give a better cut. The first barber has a unique shop that is clean and tidy. His hair is also done very nicely as well. The second barber has a chaotic, messy shop and a terrible haircut. The first shop also charges a reasonable price, while the second shop has the audacity to be slightly more expensive. What shop should he choose and why?

60. Bearded Boy

In a small town, there lived a boy and his parents. The teenaged boy, one night, asks for his parent's permission to go visit a friend nearby. They agreed that he could as long as he would be back by the time the sun rises. The boy agreed and went on his way. When he left, he had a clean-shaven face. When he returned, however, he has managed to grow a beard since the previous time he saw his parents fully. How did he manage this?

61. Anniversary Discount

As a promotional deal, a local restaurant offers a half discount to couples who dine on their anniversary. Their prices are high-end, and they want to bring in some new customers. In order to prevent any scammers from claiming the promotion when it isn't truly their anniversary, the restaurant requires proof of their wedding date. One couple happens to come in on a Thursday and forgot to bring proof. Instead of paying full price, they request to speak to the manager. The manager comes to talk with the couple and asks them to describe their wedding day. The wife answers, "Oh, it was a wonderful Sunday afternoon. The sun was shining; the birds were chirping! It was the happiest day of our lives!" The man agrees, "Yes, and it's now our 28th anniversary." The store manager denies their request as he knows now that it could not be their anniversary. How did he know this?

62. The Sheep

As shown below, when tying a sheep on one peg, it will eat a circle of grass. If he is tied to two different

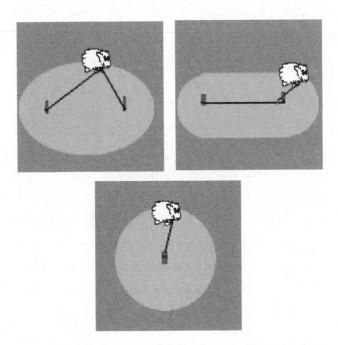

pegs, he will eat an oval. The sheep will eat in the shape of a longer oval if the rope is tightened between two pegs, connected by a ring to the rope tied to the sheep as shown below. In order to get the sheep to eat in the shape of a square, what would you need to do?

63. Wise Man

A wise man lives in a small village in his entire life. The wise man is trusted by many to give advice on their difficult problems and to settle disagreements peacefully and fairly. To test the wise man, some tourist men set out to test his abilities. Behind their back, they hold a dove so that the wise man cannot see. They then ask the wise man, "Is the dove I hold alive, or dead?" The wise man shakes his head and concludes, "I cannot answer your question correctly." Why does he say this?

64. Heaven

A man passes away and goes to heaven after the conclusion of his life. When he arrived, he was amazed to see everyone that he happened to recognize and shockingly none were wearing clothes! To his amazement, he was able to identify Adam and Eve immediately in the crowd without having any idea what they look like. How did he figure out who they were without any knowledge of their physical attributes?

65. The Concrete Room

A man stands in a room. The room has no doors or windows. The walls are also made of 6-inch thick concrete. The floor is even made of concrete. Despite this, the man is easily able to leave with ease. How does he do this?

66. Surgeon

A man and his son are driving on the highway, and they are suddenly struck by another vehicle. They swerve into the ditch, and the son is severely injured. After being rushed to the hospital, the surgeon is shocked to see the boy and exclaims, "I can't operate on this boy! He is my son!" How could this be?

67. Painted Cubes

Below, there are three different shapes containing squares. Most of the space is painted, but they all have parts that are left white. Which of the shapes are painted the most?

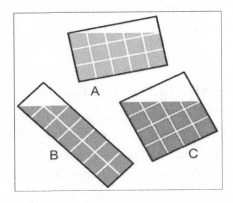

Puzzle Answers

1.   John's Trucking Disaster

Answer: Since it was Christmas Day, John's delivery trucks were not able to deliver to very many businesses as most had closed down for the day. After the driver was able to make all his stops, his truck was empty as he was not given very many supplies to transport. Since his truck was empty, his truck had a higher profile than it usually does. Due to this, the truck was able to hit a bridge it never has before on the way back.

2. Mystery Weight Loss

Answer: The enclosed room the woman enters is actually an elevator. When she presses the button, and the elevator goes into motion downward, the acceleration causes her to temporarily lower her apparent weight, effectively helping her briefly lose twenty pounds!

3. The Man In The Dark Room

Answer: The man is actually watching a movie at the movie theatre. He sips his favorite soda and subsequently chokes on a small chunk of ice. Briefly, this causes him to be unable to breathe. However, it doesn't take long before the ice melts, and he is able to return to his normal breathing.

4. The Burglar

Answer: The man walked by the two officers having already been arrested and in jail. The two officers were at the prison to get a statement from the man regarding his upcoming trial.

5. The Car Accident

Answer: All the vehicles were influenced by a child playing with his toys in his sandbox.

6. The Stranger In The Car

Answer: The man and his wife were expecting a baby. They drove to the hospital over the speed limit as she was already in labor. When they arrived, he ran to get a wheelchair to bring her into the hospital. When he returned, she had given birth to their child already.

7. Poisoned Iced Tea

Answer: The poison wasn't in the iced tea itself. It was actually in the ice cubes. Since the girl who was successfully poisoned drank so slowly, the ice had time to melt and release into her drink. As for the other girl, she drank so quickly the ice was not able to melt fast enough to release the poison.

8. Poisoned Glass

Answer: The best method is to divide the 1000 glasses into two groups of 500. Now, you must choose one of these groups and carefully pour one drop of each glass into another glass so that the 500 drops fill another glass. Now, take a sip and see if it tastes bitter in any way. If it does or doesn't, it will indicate which group of the 500 contains the poison. Once you have identified this, you may divide that group of 500 into groups of 250 and repeat the same process. You may continue doing this until you narrow it down to just one glass. This glass will contain the poison.

9. The Forgotten Book

Answer: The lady was not purchasing a book. She was actually only returning an overdue library book and paying the late fee.

10. The Twins

Answer: When Carol and Cheryl's mother went into labor, she was traveling by boat. The older twin, Cheryl, was born very early on March 1st. The boat then crossed time zones, therefore causing Carol to be born on February 28th instead. When it happens to be a leap year, the twins celebrate their birthdays two entire days apart.

11. The Cowboy

Answer: His horse's name happened also to be "Monday."

12. The Sentencing

Answer: The man could have two different appropriate responses. "It's certain that you will lock me away." You could also say, "I am lying right now."

13. Wrong Hotel Room

Answer: The woman suspected that if that man truly believed that it was his room, he would have attempted to use his key to get in, not knock! Therefore, she instantly suspects that he was attempting a robbery and was merely checking if anyone was in the room.

14. The Triangle

Answer: The image does appear like a triangle, but isn't quite a triangle. The top image has a bowed *in* hypotenuse, while the bottom image is bowed *outwards*. If you look carefully, the red and green triangles do not have the exact same ratios, resulting in different hypotenuses and a different angle, eventually resulting in that space on the bottom picture.

15. True Love At A Funeral

Answer: The woman murdered her sister in hopes that the man would return and attend the funeral so that she would be able to see him again.

16. The Murderer

Answer: The fireman happened to be the only man in the room. The rest of the poker players were, in fact, women.

17. Thirst

Answer: The man lives in a houseboat. He is currently in the middle of a saltwater ocean, unable to get fresh water.

18. Clean Faces

Answer: Tom saw Henry's clean face and assumed his face was in the same condition. The same occurred from Henry's point of view when he saw the dirty state of Tom's face.

19. Fingerprints

Answer: The man is a janitor who cleans overnight at the police station.

20. Pool Balls

Answer: The number 9 is actually supposed to be a 6 in the game of pool. By turning it around, you can use a 6, 11, and 13 to add to 30.

21. The Philosopher

Answer: Before the philosopher leaves, he winds his clock and sets it to a random time, say 9:00, for example. This is not the correct time, but it will help him estimate when he returns by tracking the amount of time his entire trip takes. As soon as he arrives, the philosopher looks at his friend's clock, which says 7:15. He stays overnight and then looks at the clock one more time before leaving. At that time it was 10:15, 15 hours later. When he returns home, his clock now says 12:40. The philosopher can now use this to subtracting the time it was when he left. He knows he has been gone for 15 hours and 40 minutes, meaning he spent 40 minutes walking and it takes him 20 minutes to walk one way. He will now know to set the time to 20 minutes after what time it was when he left his friend's house, which is 10:35.

22. Found Guilty

Answer: The accused man was the one exception of everyone that looked to the door. He was certain that she would not enter when his lawyer claimed this because he had indeed killed her.

23. Millionaire

Answer: The man started his sales as a billionaire and eventually became only a millionaire from the lost profit.

24. A Load of Wood

Answer: The wood was in the form of sawdust, therefore making it neither straight nor crooked.

25. The Short Line

In order to make the line shorter without erasing any portion of it, you can draw another line beside it, but longer. The longer line will then make the first line the shorter of the line.

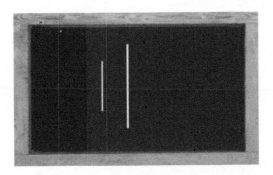

26. Rectangular House

Answer: He comes face to face with a polar bear. Only a house located in the North Pole would be able to have every side facing south.

27. Window Cleaner

Answer: The window cleaner is only cleaning the inside of the windows and therefore has no need for a safety harness.

28. Three Rooms

Answer: The second room. The Tigers have all starved to death.

29. Three Days

Answer: Yesterday, today, and tomorrow. You could also say Christmas Eve, Christmas and Boxing day or another similar combination of holidays.

30. The GoldFish

Answer: The vet was able to quickly see that the goldfish was passing away from old age. To spare the girl's feelings, he was able to switch the goldfish for a new one and return it to her.

31. Billy

Answer: Billy, as his name hints at, is, in fact, a goat. Due to this, Billy decided to eat the paper with his destination written on it. This prevents anyone from understanding where his destination is.

32. Forecast

Answer: In 72 hours, there will not even be any daylight, so it is therefore impossible to be bright and sunny.

33. East and West

Answer: If you are in the very center of the Earth's core, you would be able to look North and South, but you could not look East or West.

34. Fallen Man

Answer: While the detective was inside the building, he was able to confirm that every single window facing the man was closed. He had to open each one before throwing out his cigarette butt. Anyone that would have accidentally fallen out of the window or done this to themselves would not have closed the window behind them before their fall. The murderer must have locked it behind them.

35. The Strings

Answer: To measure exactly five minutes and thirty seconds, you will have to light both ends of the longer string first. You will allow both ends to burn consistently until they meet in the middle at five minutes. Immediately after both flames meet, you will have to do the same to the second string to measure the thirty seconds.

36. Wine Bottle

Answers: You can do this by inserting the cork into the bottle so that it is not blocking the neck. You can then shake the bottle until the coin is able to fall out.

37. The Coffee and the Fly

Answer: The woman was able to notice immediately that it was the same coffee because she had added sugar while the waitress wasn't looking. When she was given back, she sipped it and found that it was already sweet and sugar was already added.

38. Blindfolded Scott

Answer: Scott can complete the task in five rounds as follows:

Round 1: Choose any two glasses that are diagonally opposite each other. He will flip both so that they are right side up if they are not already. This will mean that at least two glasses are right side up.

Round 2: Scott will then choose two glasses that are alongside each other (adjacent). At least one will be right side up from the last round. If one of the two adjacent is upside down, turn that one right side up. There are now at least three cups right side up.

Round 3: Scott will now choose two glasses that are diagonally opposite once again. If one is turned downwards, turn it up, and all four glasses will be right side up. If both are right side up, turn one upside down, and there will be two upside-down adjacents to each other.

Round 4: Choose two adjacent glasses and flip them both. If both were the same orientation, then all four glasses will now be flipped the same way. If they were not flipped the same way, there would be two glasses that are upside down diagonally across from each other.

Round 5: Scott will choose any two glasses that are diagonally opposite and reverse both of them. All four glasses will now be the same orientation.

39. Manholes

Answer: Unlike square or rectangular covers, circular covers run no risk of sliding through the hole diagonally. Circular manhole covers can also be rolled for easy transport.

40. The Long Fishing Rod

Answer: The man was able to purchase a box from the store that was 3 x 4. He was then able to place the fishing rod inside the box diagonally to meet the bus's item length requirement.

41. The Chemist

Answer: The substances listed on the piece of paper was the chemist's clue for the officers. When combining the abbreviations of those substances, it will spell out Nicolas. His nephew is, therefore, the killer.

42. Man in the Field

Answer: The man was skydiving and his parachute failed, therefore explaining how he knew of his death moments before it happened.

43. The Wish

Answer: The manservant could tell his master this: "I wish for my mother to be able to see her grandson swing from a swingset made out of gold." Other similar answers could apply as well.

44. Mountain Trip Accident

Answer: The police found in Mr. Gold's room that he had only purchased one return plane ticket, thus suggesting that he never planned to bring his wife back home with him.

45. St. Ives

Answer: Only the one man is said to be traveling to St. Ives. He just happened to come across that man and his wives and cats on the way!

46. Equal Squares

Answer: Here are the other 8 ways to divide the square equally.

47. Truck Driver

Answer: The truck driver was walking on the side of the road and was not actually driving the wrong way on the road. Therefore, the police officer had no reason to pull him over.

48. Plane Crash

Answer: There were no survivors, and even if there were, they wouldn't bury those that were still alive!

49. Snowball

Answer: The note was a tricky clue for the man to figure out! The ? hinted that he needed to "Question Mark Smith" about the thrown snowball, meaning that Mark Smith was the culprit he was looking for!

50. The Sand Smuggler

Answer: This clever fellow is in fact smuggling bicycles! He distracts the customs officers with the simple bags of sand in order to divert their attention off of the different bikes he rides every day!

51. Guilty Husband

Answer: The police never once informed the man where the scene of the crime was. Since the man was able to bring himself to the scene of the crime without any instructions or indication of where it was confirmed that he was the one that had murdered her.

52. Who Stole the Money?

Answer: The electrician couldn't have moved the bill to between pages 2 and 3. The man checked this when the maid claimed to have wedged it between 1 and 2. With page 1 and 2 facing each other, pages 2 and 3 would not be. If the electrician was telling the truth, he would have said he moved it between pages 3 and 4. Besides, why would he move it between different pages anyway when he could have just pushed it further between the pages it was already between in the first place?

53. Two Cars

Answer: The black car was a hearse and was already carrying a dead man aboard as they were on the way to his funeral. Nobody was harmed during the accident.

54. Cell Window

Carl will be able to escape by creating a pile of dirt with his shovel. He can climb this pile in order to reach the cell window. He will then be able to climb out of the window and escape.

55. Captain's Missing Ring

Answer: The Captain knew the seaman was lying because the Japanese flag cannot be hung upside down. Only one dot is in the middle of their flag so that it can be hung in any way and still be upright.

56. First Day Of School

Answer: The police knew that the history teacher killed the science teacher because she claimed that she was giving her students a midterm test. This was not a possibility because it was the first day of the school year.

57. The Princess's Hand In Marriage

Answer: The man draws one of the papers and immediately tears it up. He then asks the King if he can see the other paper to indicate which one he pulled. The King, baffled, will take out the other paper. This will, of course, read, "Exile." This will then influence everyone to believe that the paper he initially drew would have said, "Marriage." Then the King will allow the marriage to not appear like a fool in front of his subjects.

58. Teaspoons of Sugar

Answer: You will need to put seven teaspoons in one cup. Then, you will need to put one teaspoon in one, and two in another as shown below.

59. Haircut

Answer: The second shop. It is safe to assume that usually, barbers do not attempt to cut their own hair. Even though the second barber had a messy shop, it was evident that his haircut was a reflection of the first barber's skills and the first barber had an excellent cut done by the second barber. Therefore, the second barber was the right choice. His prices are more because his quality of work is much higher.

60. Bearded Boy

Answer: The small town the family lives in is the town of Barrow in Alaska, located in the north of the United States. In this particular town, the sun sets in the middle of November and does not rise again for about 65 days. The boy is away for this entire time, and by the time he returns, he has managed to grow a beard.

61. Anniversary Discount

Answer: The store manager knew one simple fact. Every 28 years, the calendar repeats. Since it was Thursday on that particular day, he knew that it was impossible for them to have been married any day except Thursday. Still, they claimed they married on a Sunday, which therefore proved that they were lying.

62. The Sheep

Answer: In order to do this, you can install four pegs in the shape of a square, with one peg at each corner. On two sides, tighten a rope between the

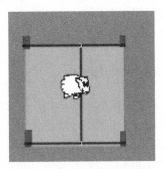

pegs, forming two lines. Use the third rope and connect it to both of the existing ropes with rings so that the sheep is secured between the two sides.

63. Wise Man

Answer: The wise man was right to answer this. It would be impossible to answer the question as the men were only there to prove him wrong and he knew this from the start. The dove was alive, but he knew if he were to answer that it was alive, they would kill it to prove him incorrect. If he said that it was dead, the dove would then be set free to prove him wrong. No matter what he answered, it could be proven wrong, so instead, he chose not to respond.

64. Heaven

Answer: The man knew it was Adam and Eve because they were the only people present that did not have a naval, meaning that they were not born from a woman's womb.

65. The Concrete Room

Answer: There are several answers that work with this scenario. First, the man is in a basement and is able to walk up the stairs to another level that has a door. The second is that the room only has three walls, so he is able to walk out. It never indicates that there are four walls. The third is that he walks out through the doorway since there is no door as it also never indicates there is no doorway where a door should be. The fourth is that he leaves through the window frame, as there is no actual window.

66. Surgeon

Answer: The surgeon also happened to be the boy's mother! It was never indicated that the surgeon was also supposedly the father.

67. Painted Cubes

Answer: All the cubes have an equal amount of space painted.

Conclusion

Thank you for making it through "67 Lateral Puzzles." Hopefully, you enjoyed the book and were able to kill some time and some boredom with the previous puzzles. Hopefully, this book was also able to help expand your mind, and open it creatively in order to solve future problems. Lateral thinking is an excellent way to do this, and we hope you continue reading and trying to solve lateral puzzles in the future. The next step to further your mind is to look for even more puzzles online, or in other books. In addition to that, we also hope that you had some fun trying to solve all of the puzzles included in this book! Thank you, everyone, for reading. Finally, if you enjoyed this book, a review on Amazon is absolutely appreciated.

Karen J. Bun

Made in the USA
Coppell, TX
21 December 2023

26723421R00038